Thoughts and Feelings

Thoughts and Feelings

Angry

Written by Susan Riley
Photos by David M. Budd

The Child's World®, Inc.

Published by The Child's World®, Inc.

Design and Production:
The Creative Spark, San Juan Capistrano, CA

Photos: © 1998 David M. Budd Photography

Library of Congress Cataloging-in-Publication Data

Riley, Susan, 1946–
     Angry / by Susan Riley.
         p. cm. — (Thoughts and feelings)
     Summary: A child explains what angers him and how he sometimes
 angers other people.
       ISBN 1-56766-667-1 (lib. reinforced : alk. paper)
      1. Anger in children Juvenile literature. [1. Anger.] I. Title. II. Series.
 BF723.A4R55   1999
 152.4′7—dc21
                                                        99-22626
                                                           CIP

I'm leaving home
as you can see.

It's because everyone is so angry at me.

Has anyone ever been angry at you? Someone gets angry at everything I do!

Mom gets angry if I spill my drink...

12

or drag in the mud,
or play in the sink.

She says, "I'm very
angry with you."
Well, sometimes
I get angry too...

like when no one listens
to what I say,
and when I can't go
with my friends to play.

I get angry when my blocks fall down, and when I can't go shopping with Mom downtown.

My sister gets
angry, too, if
I pull her hair—
and sometimes
I do!

I really can't blame her
for getting mad.

And I can't blame my sisters
or my Mom or my Dad
when they are bothered by
something I do.

I know I get

I know you do, too.

I guess getting angry
is sometimes OK,
but there's no good
reason to run away.

So I think I'll smile and
get rid of that pout.

It's time to go home and work this thing out.

For Further Information and Reading

Books

Berry, Joy Wilt. *Feeling Angry.* Scholastic Trade: 1996.

Crary, Elizabeth. *I'm Mad.* Seattle, WA: Parenting Press, 1992.

Lachner, Dorothea. *Andrew's Angry Words.* New York: North-South Books, 1997.

Web Sites

Getting the Angries Out:
http://members.aol.com/AngriesOut/

Ted the Trigger Fish Outsmarts Anger:
http://www.cts.com/crash/habtsmrt/text1.htm

Dealing with Anger: How to Keep Your Cool:
http://www.kidshealth.org/kid/feeling/anger.html

Fairy tales and stories about thoughts and feelings from all over the world: http://www.familyinternet.com/StoryGrowby/